NORTON SINGLES OHV & SV

1931 - 1966

Roy Bacon

PRC

NORTON SINGLES

First published in the United Kingdom by:
Niton Publishing
PO Box 3. Ventnor. Isle of Wight PO38 2AS

Acknowledgements
The author would like to thank those who
helped this book by supplying the photo-
graphs. Most came from the EMAP archives
or *Motor Cycle News* by courtesy of the
editor Peter Bolt. Several were kindly
supplied by the RAC and these depict the
spirit of the early postwar years well. Others
came from the Mick Woollett archive and some
from the author's files.

This edition published 1995 by
The Promotional Reprint Company Ltd,
exclusively for Selecta Book Limited,
Roundway. Devizes, Wiltshire SN10 2HR
and Reed Editions in Australia.

ISBN 1 85648 312 6

Printed in Hong Kong

The Tuck brothers, Roger and David, forcing their Big 4
Norton outfit through a section in 1988.

Contents

Introduction

The lineage of both side-valve and overhead-valve Norton singles can be traced back to the earliest days of the company. The first machine was built in 1907, while the last side-valve model, of 1954, had an engine line that was discernibly the same. The first overhead-valve engine appeared in 1922, and the last true Norton, of 1963, came from the same family tree.

The final forms of both engine types were adopted for 1931 and, such was the soundness of the designs, that minor development work kept them going for some thirty years. The remainder of the machine changed more, although the essence of the gearbox arrived in 1935 and, with minor changes, was used right through to the end of the singles line, and then on to the last twin-cylinder Norton of 1977.

The frame and cycle parts changed most of all: from girder forks and no rear suspension, via plungers, to telescopics and a pivoted rear fork, then on to the famous Featherbed frame. Details were altered to suit, and the electrics changed from magneto and dynamo to coil ignition and alternator.

For most of this period, the Norton name was kept at the forefront of the road-racing world by the camshaft singles. They dominated the 1930s, late 1940s and early 1950s, continuing to provide the bulk of the entry throughout that last decade and much of the next.

The machines covered here had no part in road-racing, but they did play an important role in off-road competition. Postwar, this led to the 500T, a model that only stayed in the range for five years, but made many friends in that short time.

The overhead- and side-valve Nortons may have lacked the glamour of the camshaft jobs, but they did a good job out on the roads. They were fast enough for their time, while the heaviest and largest of sidecars failed to have much effect on the big side-valve engine. Later, their place was taken by the vertical twins, but for many owners there was nothing to replace the thump of the single and the pull of the big flywheels.

Close-up of a 500T seen at Daytona in 1991 showing the very tight fit of the gearbox and other items.

Final design

Norton seldom changed the design of their singles, preferring to develop the originals. By 1930, however, they had become distinctly old-fashioned with an early vintage look, thanks to the long frame that was really no longer up to the job.

The 1930 range was a hotch-potch of models derived by assembling a variety of combinations from the parts available. There were two sizes of engine with side valves, two with overhead valves, two gearboxes and an assortment of frames, forks and wheels. Model numbers dated back many years, with model number 1 - also confusingly known as the 'Big 4' - dating from 1908. That machine had a 634 cc side-valve engine; other favourites were the 490 cc 16H, with side valves, and the same-capacity model 18, with ohv.

Belt drive had been dropped, but not until 1923, and some models

Pride of ownership of an early 1920s Norton. Side-valve engine lines date back to Edwardian roots and were to continue on.

The ES2 of the late 1920s with rear magneto, saddle tank and cradle frame. Changes were about to take place.

continued to use Druid side-spring forks, even in the late 1920s. For all that, the 1920s Norton with its flat tank was a highly revered machine and very popular with riders. However, the saddle tank adopted for 1929, and the cast-alloy shield fitted over the forward-mounted magneto for 1930, did little to hide the very vintage looks. It was time for Norton to make one of their rare major changes.

Two men were involved with the new design, Arthur Carroll and Edgar Franks. Carroll had joined the firm to redesign the overhead-camshaft engine for 1930; Franks assisted him in that and drew up the new models with side and overhead valves under Carroll's guidance. To all intents,

the result was the final definitive singles line.

The model line-up for 1931 differed little in type numbers from the previous year, but the machines had a new basic design which was in keeping with 1930s styling. They retained the upright engine common to all Norton singles, but had the magneto tucked in behind the engine, and switched to dry-sump lubrication. All had a shorter wheelbase and lost their spindly 1920s looks. There were to be few significant changes for a long time.

The range comprised nine models: three with side-valve engines, of two capacities, and six with ohv, of three capacities. All had a great deal in common,

The new line for 1931 with the engine revision to rear magneto and dry-sump lubrication. This is the 16H.

although two frame types - diamond and cradle - were used. All engines were of the same design, and many cycle parts were shared by most models.

The engine concept dated back to Edwardian days when James Norton, the founder, had realised the importance of providing the exhaust gases with an easy exit route, as well as the fuel mixture with an unobstructed entry. In addition, he saw the need to prevent the hot exhaust gases from heating up the engine and, hence, the need to isolate the exhaust port from the

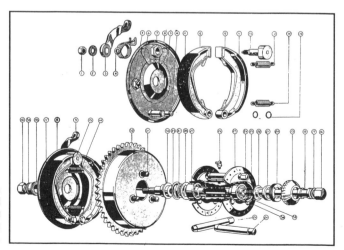

Hub and brake design adopted for 1932 and used for a very long time, both being effective.

cylinder, to keep it straight and to reduce its length. These principles were applied to the side- and overhead-valve engines in turn, providing them with a sound basis for considerable future development.

Engine dimensions were another factor that Norton seldom altered. The 490 cc engine of 1911 had bore and stroke dimensions of 79 x 100 mm, which became part of the Norton heritage, never to alter to the end of the line. Six of the 1931 machines were of this size, the 16H being the base model with side valves. A second, similar, machine was the Model 2, which was simply the 16H with footboards and a change of handlebars to what were listed as 'semi-TT bars'.

The other four 490 cc models all had overhead valves, the model 18 being the most basic. The model 20 was an 18 with a twin-port cylinder head, while the ES2 was a model 18 in a cradle frame; the model 22 being a twin-port version of the ES2. Of the remaining models, the Big 4 had a 634 cc side-valve engine with 82 x 120 mm dimensions, while the other two were smaller and larger ohv versions of the 18. The JE, of 348 cc, had dimensions of 71 x 88 mm, and the model 19, of 588 cc, had dimensions of 79 x 120 mm, combining the bore of the 490 cc engine with the stroke of the Big 4.

All engines were based on a simple cast-aluminium crankcase, split on the vertical centre-line with a spigot diameter to locate the two halves. A small sump was formed at the rear of the base to act as a collection point for the lubricating oil, and a knife edge just above it helped remove oil from the flywheels. Full-width bosses enabled the engine plates to be well clamped to the assembled crankcase, the studs used holding the crankcase halves together at the same time.

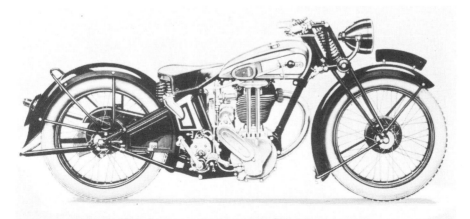

The Model 18 for 1933, still with the left-hand exhaust system and awkward toolbox with its top hinge.

The top of the crankcase was machined flat and provided with four studs to secure the barrel, this item being spigoted into the crankcase mouth. The timing chest and oil pump mounting were included in the right-hand crankcase casting, there being a single timing cover.

Two good-sized main bearings supported the built-up crankshaft, which had the mainshafts pressed into the large, heavy flywheels. The crankpin was a taper-fit into each flywheel, being pulled up by a nut on each side. This nut was locked by a small screw inserted into one of two holes. Shoulders were incorporated

pin, which was retained in the piston by circlips. All pistons had three rings (two compression and one scraper), the piston crowns being flat or domed to suit the engine type and compression ratio. Each piston ran in a cast-iron barrel whose crankcase spigot was relieved locally in the bore to clear the connecting rod.

Side-valve engines had the barrel extended out to the right for the valves and ports. Each valve moved in a pressed-in guide and was controlled by a single spring that was retained by a collar and collets. A simple bracket, fitted to the top of

Model 19 as for 1934, a larger single with even more pulling power.

in the crankpin, which was hardened between them on the roller track.

The big-end comprised a double row of uncaged rollers, which ran directly on the crankpin, but in a hardened ring that was pressed into the big-end eye of the connecting rod. The small-end was bushed for the hollow, fully-floating gudgeon

the crankcase between the valves, carried a lever to lift the exhaust valve plus a return spring. Both valves were concealed by a simple pressed cover that was retained by a single thumb-screw. The inlet tract was screwed into the port, while the exhaust pipe was a push-fit. The cylinder head was cast in iron and

The Amal carburettor and Lucas mag-dyno were familiar sights by 1934 when this 16H was built. Earlier gearbox type.

held down on a gasket by nine nuts on studs. There was a blanking plug over the piston so that the ignition timing could be set from the piston position without removing the head, while the sparking plug went above the inlet valve.

For the overhead-valve engine, the cylinder was a simple casting whose fins were only interrupted by the cut-outs for the pushrod tubes. The cylinder head was equally straightforward and was held in place, without a gasket, by four sleeve nuts, to which the rocker box was bolted. The valve guides were pressed in but, unlike the side-valve model, twin springs were used to control each valve. The inlet tract was screwed into the port with a locknut to secure it, but the exhaust port was threaded for a finned nut which secured the pipe. Over the years, many owners were to have to work at keeping that nut tight.

The rocker box was cast in aluminium with a detachable cover held to the right-hand side by six screws. Both cover and rocker box side were formed to clamp a seal to the top of each pushrod tube. The lower end of each plated tube was fixed to a union by a large nut, the union being screwed into the top face of the crankcase.

Each rocker spindle was forged in one with its right-hand arm, this arm fitting into the top of the pushrod and being enclosed by the side cover. Both rockers oscillated in grease-lubricated bushes, and each had a second arm located to the left-hand end of the spindle by key and taper, a nut holding the assembly together. This second arm, which opened the valve, was external to the rocker box, as were valves, springs and guides. Thus, all were

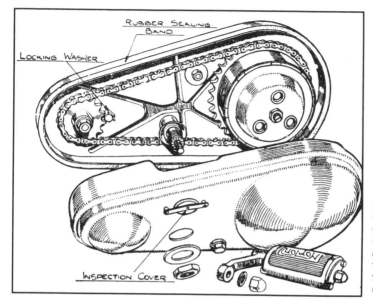

Rubber Sealing Band

Locking Washer

Inspection Cover

Norton pressed-steel primary chaincase with rubber sealing band and single nut outer fixing. Worked well for many years unless abused.

subject to the effects of wind and weather.

Within the timing chest, there was a cam and follower for each valve. In the side-valve engines, the followers moved tappets in guides that were screwed into the crankcase, each tappet incorporating a valve gap adjuster at its top end. For the ohv engines, a different type of follower was used to accept the lower pushrod end. Each cam was formed in one with its shaft and driving gear, the latter meshing with a pinion keyed to the crankshaft. The shafts turned in bronze, shouldered bushes fitted in the crankcase and the timing cover, while further bushes, similarly fitted, served the cam followers.

The timing chest extended down below the cams to encompass the oil pump, which was bolted to a flat face within the chest. The pump was driven by a worm wheel, which was screwed on to the end of the crankshaft with a left-hand thread. This also held the timing pinion in place. Lubrication was by the dry-sump system using a duplex-gear pump. Carroll had intended to use the camshaft-engine pump, which was housed in a circular body that was a close-tolerance fit in a bored crankcase hole. Franks argued that, for production, a flat surface would be much easier to machine, so the famous Norton gear pump was born.

The pump was simple enough: a body recessed on each side for the two gear pairs, covers for each end, gear spindles and a drive pinion. It worked well and, from then on, was used by the firm for the singles and, in a modified form, for the postwar twins. Abingdon made the pumps,

The 1934 ES2 with its overhead valves, slim pushrod tubes and cradle frame.

which proved tolerant of the fit of the worm drive that looked as if it could vary too much, but in practice, it worked well. The only fault was a tendency for the oil to drain through the pump and into the sump if the machine was left standing for too long. Norton maintained that this did not happen, but owners found

that it did, and some fitted an anti-drain ball valve at the tank connection.

Oil from the pump was sent via a sealing nipple into the timing cover, where a relief valve controlled the pressure and returned the excess to the timing chest. A plunger tell-tale, in the top edge of the timing cover,

The gearbox adopted by Norton for 1935 with upright end cover. The essentials were to live on into the 1970s on the twins.

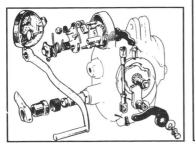

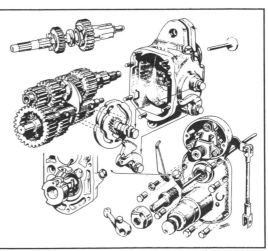

let the rider know that all was well with the system. The drillings in the cover led the oil to a spring-loaded jet, which fed into the end of the crankshaft and, hence, via drillings, to the big-end. This was fed from the side, there being no drilled holes in the crankpin. The system was completed by a take-off which fed oil to the rear of the cylinder wall. At first, this incorporated a screw adjuster, but it was soon changed to a fixed supply. On the return side, the oil simply drained down to the crankcase sump, from where it went to the scavenge pump and, thus, back to the oil tank. There was just one filter in the system, this being fitted to the feed line at the tank.

The timing cover was extended up and to the rear to enclose the chain drive to the Lucas magneto, which had a third-brush-type dynamo strapped to its back. The drive was taken from the inlet camshaft, which extended through the timing cover to carry a small sprocket on its end. This matched the one on the magneto, which was mounted on a platform behind the cylinder, where its position was adjustable to set the chain tension. Once this had been done, the chain was enclosed by an outer cover that was held to the timing cover by two screws.

All models had an Amal carburettor to supply the mixture, and Norton managed to cover the range with just two sizes of the Type 6 instrument. This had a separate float chamber which was on the left of the mixing chamber in all cases. From the exhaust port, the pipe and silencer went to the left of the machine as standard, the extra

Competition option as offered for 1935 with knobbly tyres, slim mudguards and more ground clearance.

The Models 50 and twin-port 55 were built from 1933 as 348 cc editions of the larger machines. This is the 1935 Model 55.

system for twin-port models being added on the right. The nearside positioning allowed an easy sweep for the exhaust pipe of the ohv models, but for the side-valve machines, it meant that the pipe had to curl round and across in front of the crankcase.

A cam-lobe shock absorber, on the left-hand end of the crankshaft, drove the Sturmey Archer clutch and gearbox by a single-strand chain under a pressed-steel cover. All models had a three-speed gearbox and hand-change, this being controlled by a lever mounted on the right-hand side of the petrol tank. There were options of alternative ratios and four speeds, but the hand-change was retained for these. As well as the crankshaft-mounted shock absorber, there was a further shock absorber built into the clutch centre, this using rubber buffers as

the absorbent medium. The clutch itself ran dry and was a multi-plate type with Ferodo friction inserts, the plates being clamped by six springs.

All models, except the ES2, had a diamond frame constructed in the traditional way, using tubes that were pinned and brazed into forged lugs. There were single top, down and seat tubes to form the main section, with upper and lower chainstays on each side to the rear. The result was simple, but strong. The down tube had lugs at its lower end to bolt to the front of the crankcase, while plates joined the engine to the gearbox and that assembly to the seat tube and rear frame.

For the ES2 and model 22, there was a cradle frame in which the down tube extended to the cradle beneath the crankcase, the two being bolted together. The seat tube was also extended to mate with the junction of cradle and lower chainstays, the result being an even more rigid frame.

Norton girder front forks with built-in friction dampers, based on the Webb type, were fitted to all frames. A steering damper went below the headstock, with the control knob above it, while fork movement was controlled by a single, central spring. Norton and Webb hubs were used for the front wheels, and Enfield for the rear, the rear brake being on the right-hand side and, thus, remote from the sprocket. All brakes were of the single-leading-shoe type, and all

tyres 26 x 3.25 in. - the combination of outside diameter and section being the method used to classify tyres in those days.

The cycle parts of all models were much the same, although the oil tank of the ES2 and model 22 differed from the other models, being the same as that used by the camshaft machines. It remained in the same place, however - below the saddle on the right-hand side, matched on the left by the battery. A luggage grid went behind the saddle and had leather-faced toolboxes hanging from each side. A pillion pad could be added if desired.

Both mudguards were in steel and of a heavy section, the tail of the

A 1938 Big 4 and Norton Model G sidecar outfit during a road test conducted that year.

rear one being removable to allow the wheel to be withdrawn. The Lucas headlamp was carried by mountings fixed to the forks and had the light switch mounted in the rear of its shell and the ammeter in its top. There was a rear stand, and a saddle tank for the petrol. Finish was black for nearly all parts, but both the petrol and oil tanks were in silver with the traditional Norton lining of a wide black outer stripe and a thin red inner stripe.

Thus, the new Norton design went out to battle for sales in the depressed days of the early 1930s.

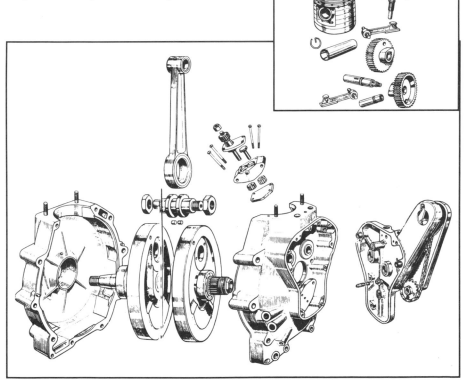

Exploded drawing of the 16H engine in its 1938 form with enclosed valve gear. The bottom half of the ohv engine was virtually the same, just the cam followers differing.

The Thirties

Times became worse before they improved, so firms had to cut as many corners as possible on the one hand, while offering something to whet the appetite of anyone who looked remotely like a customer. This led most to produce large ranges from a small number of basic parts with plenty of options to suit all tastes.

At Norton, this policy kept the Model 2 in the range for 1932, despite the fact that it was simply a 16H with footboards and a change of bars. No doubt, you could have had it with the optional four speeds and foot-change if you wished, all for just over £50 in those tough times. Out

from the range went the models 22 and JE, but that still left seven to choose from.

The main change for all models was to Norton's own quickly-detachable and interchangeable wheels, a type that was to run on for many years in the postwar era. Each hub had simple flanges for the spokes and was secured to the brake drum by three long sleeve nuts that ran through one flange to clamp the other. The brakes became a type which also remained in use for a long time. Each of the single leading shoes was in light-alloy and had its own pivot pin, which gave the shoe excellent support. Some owners

Model 50 for 1938 with the strange silencer fitted to all Nortons that year - and that year only!

A 1939 ES2 as seen in California many years later.

would bridge the pins at their outer ends, and this minor modification made an excellent brake even better.

The brakes worked in 7 in. malleable iron drums, the rear drum being integral with its sprocket. This was narrower than usual with a chain size of 5/8 x 1/4 in. - another Norton feature that was to last for many years, up to 1964 in fact. It seemed that the iron of the sprocket gave the hardened rollers of the chain an easy time, to their mutual benefit and reduced wear.

Other 1932 changes were to a steel toolbox, which was fitted between the chainstays on the right-hand side, but with the lid hinged from the top and the catch at the bottom. This meant that the lid had to be held or tied up when working on the machine - hardly an asset, especially in the dark. The rear carrier became an option, one item in a list of some length. For the side-

valve models, the silencer was moved over to the right-hand side, which allowed the exhaust pipe to follow a much simpler sweep to it. On the Model 19, the cylinder studs were lengthened to run up through the head so that the sleeve nuts held both head and barrel in place.

The Model 19 was altered further for 1933 when its bore and stroke dimensions became 82 x 113 mm and the capacity was increased to 597 cc. That year saw the Model 2 dropped, but there were two new additions in the form of the Models 50 and 55. Both had overhead-valve engines of 348 cc capacity with dimensions of 71 x 88 mm, the Model 55 having a twin-port head. Thus, the two newcomers mirrored the existing 18 and 20 models, other than in capacity and gearing. However, they did have through-studs to secure the head and barrel, as on the Model 19. For all models,

The Model 18 for 1939. Still 490 cc, diamond frame and the features of the 1930s.

the carburettor material changed from brass to die-cast alloy so the Amal type number became 76.

All the ohv models were fitted with the four-speed gearbox with hand-change as standard, foot operation remaining an option. For the 16H and Big 4, the three speeds continued as standard, but the other options remained. The wheel hubs were amended with plated end caps, and the finish was brightened with chrome-plating for all petrol and oil tanks. Upswept, waist-level exhaust pipes were offered, at no extra charge, for any ohv model.

A second drive-side main bearing was added to all engines for 1934, when the timing gears were revised to run as a train from crankshaft to exhaust to inlet. The new gear arrangement was supposed to reduce engine noise, but its more noticeable effect was to reverse the

For lovers of the side-valve engine, there was the 16H of 1939 with the same cycle parts as the ohv models.

1946 Norton PROGRAMME

At the end of August we complete our contracts for the Services. (Remember: One in Every Four was a NORTON!)

All our efforts will then be directed towards supplying Export and Home demands.

We start with two models: 16H (490 c.c. side-valve) and 18 (490 c.c. o.h.v. illustrated below). **They will continue unchanged during 1946.**

Both models 16H and 18 will incorporate the famous NORTON cradle frame; the usual NORTON finish, with all the usual plated parts in chromium finish. Other modifications will include: improved type silencer; all-ground timing gears; enclosed clutch worm in gearbox, etc.

Ask your NORTON dealer for a copy of our ADVANCE FOLDER giving illustrations and full details of these two machines.

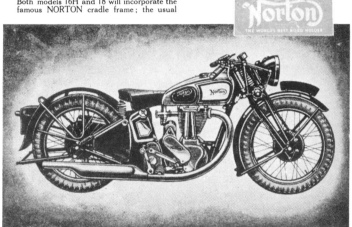

After the war the Model 18 went into the cradle frame but retained the girder forks for a short while. August 1945 advertisement.

direction of rotation of the magneto to clockwise, which was unusual for a motorcycle. For the ohv engines, small pipes were added to carry lubricant from the rocker box to each valve guide.

The primary transmission underwent major changes that year with the removal of the engine shock absorber, a switch to the Norton clutch and the appearance of the Norton oil-bath chaincase. For the first, the sprocket became plain and was fixed to a taper, being secured by a nut. The clutch was to work well and play its part in the good Norton gearchange to come, while the oil-bath chaincase was to be used for many years.

The clutch was a multi-plate type with a shock-absorber based on rubber buffers built into its centre. It was clamped by three springs, while the friction plates were fitted with Ferodo inserts developed to run in oil. Despite this, the drum had a band fitted around it to prevent too much oil from reaching the friction surfaces. The pressure plate was lifted by a large-diameter mushroom, which ensured that it lifted squarely so that the clutch plates could separate easily, assisting the gearchange.

The chaincase design was simple. It comprised an inner pressing with a ledge running round it, close to its outer edge. A wide rubber band

The ES2 returned to the range for 1947 with Roadholder telescopics and plunger rear suspension. A few were built for 1946 but not listed.

went over the ledge, while the outer cover was fitted over both to seal against the band. One large nut, fitted to the footrest hanger, held the outer cover in place, and the seal worked well, provided the nut was not over-tightened. An inspection cap allowed both the chain tension to be checked and oil to be added.

In addition to the transmission changes, the gearbox was fitted with a neater positive-stop change mechanism, and the front forks became the Norton type with extra check springs. These forks had been introduced for the camshaft models in the previous year and differed from earlier types in having a check spring fitted between forward extensions of the fork links on each side. These extensions were designed to supplement the main spring, their action being more pronounced at the extremes of fork movement. The new design

continued to mount the headlamp on two prongs that were fitted into the lower spindle housing of the fork, this system having been adopted for 1932.

The final major transmission change came in 1935 with the adoption of the four-speed Norton gearbox by all models. This came about because Raleigh, who had been making the gearboxes used by Norton and others under the Sturmey Archer name, left the motorcycle market in 1934 and ceased gearbox production. Having used Sturmey gearboxes since they moved from direct belt drive, Norton were not keen on fitting Albion or Burman boxes, so they took over the design and had it made for them by Burman.

Before manufacture of the Norton gearbox began, the design was amended in minor ways to improve the bearings and the positive-stop mechanism. Otherwise, it continued as a straightforward design in the British fashion, the mainshaft being above the layshaft and concentric with the sleeve gear. Both clutch and final drive were on the left; the sliding gears which selected the ratios were controlled by two forks and a circular camplate; and the positive-stop mechanism was in a housing in the top of the gearbox end cover. From there, it was connected by a linkage to the camplate gear and moved by a lengthy gear pedal. The kickstart lever went on the right, below the gear pedal, and between them was located the quick-thread clutch-lift mechanism.

Other changes for 1935 were to tubular silencers - now on the right for the ohv models - rubber-mounted handlebars with tidied-up controls,

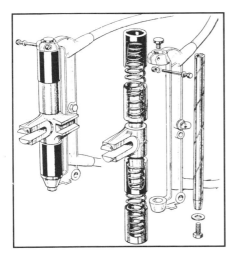

Details of the Norton plunger rear suspension used from 1947 to 1952 for singles and twins.

a speedometer drive facility in the front hub, and chrome-plated wheel rims with red-lined, black centres. The tank lining reversed to put the thin red line outside the thicker black one. A centre stand was provided in addition to the rear one, but was designed to act as a prop stand. Thus, it did not lift either wheel clear of the ground, but it did support the machine when lent to either side. Competition versions of any model could be had for an extra £5, for which the owner received a special frame to increase ground clearance, narrower front fork and wheel hub, competition tyres on chrome-plated wheel rims, narrow mudguards, a high-level exhaust system and a folding kickstart.

There were few changes for 1936, the model range being unaltered. For the 490 cc ohv engines, there were through-studs to secure the head and barrel, bringing them into line with the 19, 50 and 55 models. The oil circulation rate was increased and, thanks to this, fatter pushrod tubes were fitted, which looked better than the earlier spindly ones. Elsewhere, the hub covers were dropped, as they had not proved too successful, and the toolbox hinge was moved to the bottom, which pleased owners. The petrol tank was new, being wider at the nose, and deeper, than before.

Even less happened for 1937. Changes were limited to 14 mm plugs for the ohv engines and a switch to compensated voltage control for the electrics. This control box was fixed

Model 18 from 1947 out in California some 40 years later with a 1930s ES2 standing behind it.

to one of the upper chainstays. The riding position was improved with new handlebars, which swept back more, and a lower saddle height. Oil tanks were increased in size without becoming obtrusive.

For 1938, there were some changes to the engines: the valves were fully enclosed, and the cams and their followers modified.

Valve enclosure introduced a new ohv cylinder head with a well for each valve. Above each well there was a distance piece, cast to match the outline, and the new rocker box went on top of these. Each rocker became an assembly comprising a shaft that oscillated in a single bush and arms that were fitted on keyed tapers at the ends.

The rocker box fitted over the wells to enclose them and extended to the right where a cover plate was fitted. The pushrod tubes were angled inwards at the top, but were

retained, as before, by union nuts and the rocker box side cover-plate. This plate had a further access cover fitted to it, as the valve gap adjustment was made at the top of each pushrod and the cover enabled it to be set. On the side-valve engines, enclosure was achieved by extending the cylinder casting around the parts, leaving an air gap between the resulting chamber and the cylinder. An alloy lid, retained by a single fixing, completed the job.

For all engines, there were wider cams, flat cam followers and an improved lubrication system. The oil tell-tale was deleted as part of this change. Finally, all models were fitted with a new silencer, known at the works as 'the cow's udder'. This had twin tail pipes exiting from a deep body. It was not an attractive sight.

All models went back to the

tubular silencer for 1939, when the ES2 had two options listed for it - both from the camshaft models. One was a frame with plunger rear suspension in which the load and rebound springs were enclosed, but undamped. When this was supplied, the rear wheel was no longer quickly detachable, as its single spindle had to help tie the two plunger sliders together. With this frame came an odd rear stand which pivoted from the lower chainstays just below the spring boxes and faced forward. If it dropped it made a great sprag but really was a lethal feature. The other option was the camshaft machines' petrol tank, which gave an improved appearance.

There were to have been a good few changes for 1940: revised engine dimensions, an altered gearbox end, cradle frames for all, and the option of telescopic front forks. None came to pass, however, as the firm was already well committed to service contracts for more mundane machines; civilian production simply came to an end.

An early postwar Model 18 or ES2 in a workshop for minor attention while 16H Nortons, most likely ex-wd, are rebuilt on the benches.

The 16H in its 1948 form with the 'chimney-pot' valve enclosure adopted that year along with a light-alloy cylinder head.

Norton Big 4 plus Watsonian Warwick sidecar leaving Bude with a load of four heavy men during a press test run in 1949.

Wartime

War came as no surprise to those who read their newspapers in the late 1930s, so Norton had already made their preparations during this period. They saw a need for simple, basic military motorcycles and went to some lengths to ensure that they would be among the firms supplying them. Thus, it came about that the firm was awarded a contract to produce large numbers of the 16H model.

In essence, the machine selected was the 1937 type with open valve gear, as this model had run in various service tests, and the later version with enclosed valves had not. The Services, and the War Office in particular, were not known for buying anything that had not been tried and tested to the utmost.

Little had to be altered to suit military use, but the trials frame was used to house the mechanics, as this gave a little more ground clearance. An undershield was added to protect the crankcase and assist the machine to slide over obstacles. Trials forks, which had built-in buffer stops, were fitted, along with standard wheels, front and rear.

Drive-side of a 1949 ES2, much as it was ten or more years earlier except for the suspension.

A charming period scene near Dorking in the early 1950s. The RAC patrol man is talking to A

mpson, the RAC motorcycle manager of those days.

Restored 500T in very nice order. There should be a toolbox above the right-side upper chainstay.

The rest of the machine was essentially standard, but altered to cheapen production where this could be done. Thus, the prewar option of a tank-top instrument panel was not used. Either a standard toolbox was fitted, or a new one that was mounted high on the right; there was a rear carrier, and a pillion pad could be added. In time, the standard Norton footrests were replaced by simpler items, the handlebar grips became webbing, and a smaller headlight was fitted.

For overseas use, an air filter was added, but the stylish prewar service type (mounted above the right-hand pillion rest) soon gave way to a crude box on top of the petrol tank. Colours varied to suit the service supplied, as some went to the RAF, but most were in some shade of army khaki or desert sand.

In this way, the 16H went to war, around 100,000 being supplied in

all. Faults there were, for the gearchange linkage wore, the gearbox lugs could break, the magneto work loose on its platform, and the rear wheel nuts disappear. What mattered was that none of these problems stopped a dispatch rider from jury-rigging a repair to get back to base. None liked the alternative of walking, their job breeding more self-confidence and ability to cope than was usual for military men.

During their service life, the machines were usually rebuilt more than once with scant regard for keeping original parts together. Colours could, and did, change depending on what paint was available, and postwar, many were quickly painted black and sold to a transport-hungry public by enterprising dealers. They served well during that period, being backed by the extensive spares holdings that also came on to the market.

Once the 16H contract was in the bag, Norton began to push the Ministry for another to build sidecar outfits for the motorised cavalry. The firm had experience of what was needed, as they had built trials outfits with sidecar wheel drive in the late 1930s, so they knew the problems and their solutions.

For the outfit, they took the 634 cc Big 4 in its 1938 form with enclosed valves, added a sidecar based on the standard Norton chassis, and modified the result to include the drive to the sidecar wheel. To this end, the rear fork ends of the frame were enlarged to create bearing housings for the wheel spindle. This

Showing the tight fit of the 500T engine into the frame, this one being assembled in California.

drove a simple dog clutch, controlled by a hand lever, with a drive shaft from this to the sidecar wheel. It meant that the sidecar wheel could not lead the rear one, as is usual for outfits, but the frame alterations did provide space for a 4.00 in. section trials-type rear tyre.

The Norton sidecar chassis supported the wheel spindle on both sides, so it avoided the stresses applied to the more-usual stub axle arrangement. There was also an outer chassis tube to protect the wheel and ward off obstacles. Bearings in the lugs made the spindle a live type and, as the hub was common to the machine, all three wheels could be interchanged, while one spare fitted all locations.

The sidecar body was sparse, crude and strong. There was a seat, a stowage box at the rear, a front panel and grab handles. A simple mudguard was fitted over the sidecar wheel, but that for the front wheel was wider than normal so that the girder forks passed through it. Large valances were normally fitted to the front mudguard.

Some outfits were fitted with platform sidecars to carry ammunition, a machine gun on a mounting, or a mortar. Regardless of equipment, tests soon showed that the Big 4 was not really up to pulling it all along, so the engine was modified to increase its power. This was done with a new top half, in which the combustion chamber was positioned mainly over the valves, so the engine ceased to be fully of the 1938 type.

Bottom yoke of a 500T, seen at Daytona in 1991, showing the way the fork legs were pulled back.

Several thousand outfits were built and served at home and in North Africa. This experience suggested that more power would help and led to a prototype with a V-twin engine, but then the Jeep arrived from the USA. This was much more suited to general army use, so the outfits were dropped, for they required real skill to get the best from them.

Norton had one other wartime single, which was built to a War Office specification calling for low weight. To meet this, the firm used an all-alloy side-valve engine, of 348 cc, in a welded frame with a number of light-alloy details. A batch of 50 was made, but nearly all went to France and were abandoned during the Dunkirk retreat.

After that, maximum production took priority, so Norton got on with making the 16H in large numbers; no one having much time for experiments. However, one that did happen was the fitment, to a 16H, of telescopic front forks developed from the prewar racing type, but with hydraulic damping. After the war, they became the famous Roadholders.

Postwar days

Maximum production continued to be essential once the war was over, as the government was crying out for exports to pay the bills. The public was desperate for transport of any kind so, for Norton, the position was simple. They changed the paint colour from khaki to black and continued to build the 16H.

In fact, they did make some changes. The engines followed the 1939 style with enclosed valves, and the frame was the full-cradle type, as used by the prewar ES2. They also built the ohv model 18, which was nearly identical. The models continued to be fitted with girder forks, while a minor change was to add an outer end cover to the gearbox to enclose the clutch mechanism and smooth the lines. Other alterations were minimal: the headlamp held by stays, a larger toolbox, and revised silencer and

Big 4 hitched to a Canterbury Vicking sidecar in 1952 when the tank finish was more austere.

The ES2 in its first pivoted-fork frame as first seen in 1953.

oil tank. The finish was as in the past, mainly black, the petrol and oil tanks being chrome-plated with silver panels lined in black and red, the red now the inner line once again. Wheel rims were chrome-plated with black centres, lined in red.

There were no changes for 1946, but there were for 1947 when the ES2 and Big 4 returned to the range. In fact, although not listed, some ES2 machines were built late in 1946 and numbered as for that model year. All four models were fitted with the hydraulically-damped Roadholder telescopic front forks. The top bridge of the fork was used to carry the speedometer, but the ammeter and light switch remained in their small panel in the back of the headlamp shell.

The ES2 was fitted with plunger rear suspension as standard, but this remained without damping. The Big 4 was given the engine top half that had been developed for the wartime sidecar outfit, but otherwise it was as before. Both side-valve models, the 16H and Big 4, were to remain listed in the rigid frame only, but a few were built with plunger rear suspension.

Again unlisted, but built in very small numbers for 1947, were the 350 and 500 Trials models. These used the all-iron engine from the prewar model 50 or model 18, the wartime 16H frame, Roadholder forks and suitable gearing, tyres and mudguards. There was a 21 in. front wheel and a high-level exhaust system as a concession to the intended use, but otherwise the models came with the standard full electrics and cycle parts, so they were far too heavy for their job. They were not available for long.

The engines had a number of changes for 1948, mainly affecting the timing chest and valve enclosure. The cam followers were replaced by tappets with flat feet, which allowed the chest to be made smaller. Internally, the flywheels had their diameter reduced, which permitted the use of a longer piston skirt. Both the magneto sprockets gained a tooth, which was sneaky. It meant that later rebuilds using odd spares would fire once - and then not for some time!

For the side-valve engines, there was a new, light-alloy casting to enclose the valves, so there was no longer any need for the chamber cast on the side of the cylinder. The new casting was fitted between the crankcase and the barrel, with sealing washers at each end, and looked like a pair of chimney pots rising from a chamber. This chamber was open to give access to the adjusters in the tappet tops, being sealed by a cover that was held in place by a single nut. Light-alloy cylinder heads replaced the old iron ones for the side-valve machines. The engine dimensions of the Big 4 were altered to 82 x 113 mm, and its capacity to 597 cc.

The same general changes applied to the ohv engine, which had a new, one-piece rocker box with a single side cover to give access to the

Side-valve single, either a 16H or a Big 4, fitted with the saddle that riders preferred for a rigid frame.

adjusters in the tops of the pushrods. The new rocker box had fixed spindles and bushed, one-piece rockers, but otherwise it was much as before, the pushrod tubes being fitted between the box and the crankcase against end seals. The rockers were lubricated by a feed taken from the main oil return pipe, and the oil drained back via the pushrod tubes or holes drilled through the head and barrel from the valve wells.

Little was altered on the existing models for 1949, but they were joined by an important new machine, the 500T, built for trials use. This was destined to be very popular in its field at the time, and to remain so for many years after production ceased.

The 500T was the result of work carried out by the clever McCandless brothers, more widely known for the Featherbed frame. They wanted to build a better trials Norton, and began with the wartime 16H frame, to reduce both the weight and length, before moving on to the front forks. These started as the standard Roadholders, but in that form carried the front wheel too far ahead. The brothers simply cut and welded the fork yokes to reposition the legs and wheel further to the rear, thus reducing the wheelbase and markedly improving the handling in trials sections.

This was the basis of the 500T, which was fitted with a 490 cc engine with an all-alloy top half and a 6.0:1 compression ratio, but otherwise it was as that used by the ES2 and model 18. The cylinder head was bi-metal, while the barrel was linered, but the cams and flywheels were stock. The result was plenty of low-

Final 16H and Big 4 year was 1954 when they were fitted with an 8 in. front brake and still had their original engine line.

The RAC used Norton outfits to patrol the roads for many years and by 1955 were equipped with Model 19 singles.

down plonk, plus immediate power when required - well, until the carburettor slide wore. Then the response was either as usual or it spat-back and the effect was not so dramatic!

The carburettor was the same Amal 276 as used by the road models, while the exhaust ran down, under the timing chest and kickstart spindle, and then up a little to a tilted silencer. The gearbox had the prewar type of end-cover and tucked into the small space left between the back of the crankcase and the rear wheel. It contained wide ratios, while the end cover was modified to reduce its size and tuck in the kickstart spindle boss. The lever

itself folded.

The whole assembly was a tight fit in the frame, so tight, in fact, that it was not possible to remove the rocker box without taking the engine out. As the box had to come off to enable the head nuts to be tightened, it was no easy task to keep the head joint gas- and oil-tight.

Features and fittings were in the style of the times. The oil tank was on the right-hand side, under the nose of a Dunlop rubber saddle. There was a small toolbox on the same side, above the top chainstay, while a shield protected the crankcase. Narrow, light-alloy mudguards, finished in black, were fitted along with a good prop stand

This rigid Model 19R was only listed for 1955.

and a rear stand which most owners soon discarded.

The front brake remained at 7 in., but it differed in that it had a scalloped hub and an alloy brake plate, which was ribbed to the cam spindle boss and had a water-excluding ring. The petrol tank was in steel with a capacity of 2-1/2 gallons, while its mounting was by two prongs at the front and a single rear bolt. Rubber insulation protected it from vibration and strain without impeding the ease with which it could be removed.

Ignition was by a racing BTH magneto, and an optional lighting set was spoken of, but was not to be found in Lucas lists. The wheels carried competition tyres on high-tensile steel rims, the front size being 2.75 x 21 in., and the rear 4.00 x 19 in. A Manx rev-counter mounting held the speedometer neatly in the fork top-yoke, just behind the competition number plate.

Finish for the 500T was mainly black with polished lower fork legs and dull chrome-plating for the petrol tank. This was relieved by a silver top panel, lined in red and black, the whole ensemble having very smart lines.

The Norton singles experienced few changes in the early 1950s, but one major alteration was to the gearbox in 1950. Much of the assembly stayed as it was, but the positive-stop mechanism was positioned ahead of the end cover, which was extended forwards to enclose it. This allowed the mechanism to be linked more directly to the camplate and placed the gear pedal in a much better position - lower and with a reduced travel.

Other 1950 changes saw the

dynamo control unit moved into the toolbox out of the weather, a longer rear chainguard, and a prop stand for the ES2. The last was bolted to the front engine plate on the left-hand side of the machine. For the 500T, however, the gearbox type remained unchanged, as the newer unit could not be fitted due to the lack of space, but its first gear ratio was raised a little. For all models, the finish continued as before.

Prop stands appeared for all the other road models in 1951, a year when the petrol tanks were enlarged, new oil tanks fitted and a die-cast, light-alloy brake backplate appeared for the front wheel. The 500T lost its hub scallops and, due to the nickel shortage, the tank finish for all models became silver, the panels being outlined in red and black lining.

There were no changes for 1952, except to the black lining of the road model's petrol tanks, which became much thinner, while the wheel rim finish was changed to silver centres lined in red. More happened for 1953, when the ES2 was given a new frame, each rigid-frame road model was fitted with a dualseat, and all models had a larger, red plastic rear lamp.

Another Model 19S of the RAC with the rider in discussion with Aubrey Thompson who sits on a Dominator Model 7 twin.

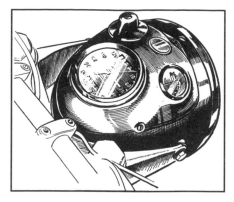

The deeper headlamp shell with separate panel for speedometer, ammeter and light switch used for 1956. Integral for 1957.

The frame for the ES2 had pivoted-fork rear suspension, controlled by Girling units, but it was not the Featherbed duplex type that buyers would have preferred. Instead, it had a single downtube and was constructed in the traditional way, using forged lugs into which the various tubes were brazed. Effectively, the front end was as before, while the rear portion was new and some details had been re-arranged. A dualseat was fitted, the horn moved into the sub-frame corner, behind the oil tank, and the silencer was altered to a pear shape. The exhaust pipe was of smaller bore, an underslung pilot lamp appeared on the headlamp shell, and the gearing had been altered slightly.

Finish for the ES2 was in black, while the tank was chrome-plated with silver panels, lined in black and red. The wheel rims were chrome-plated with silver centres, lined in red. The same finish was adopted

by the model 18. The two side-valve machines had the same rim finish, but kept the all-silver tank colour with panels outlined in black and red lining.

For 1954, an 8 in. front brake was listed for all models, but it is thought that, in fact, this did not apply to the 500T. Certainly, a trials machine would not have required such a fitting, and the listing was a general one in the brochure. However, it appears that some buyers did insist on having the listed 8 in. brake, but this would have been easy enough for a dealer to arrange, so both sizes are known to have existed on the 500T. In the same way, the brochure indicates a change to a Lucas magneto, but this is not supported by the Lucas lists. Otherwise, there was no change, and the finish for the range continued as before.

There was one new machine for 1954, but only as a prototype and in a new capacity for Norton, this being 250 cc. The machine was built in 1953 and had a high-camshaft, overhead-valve engine, which was inclined forwards a little. Engine dimensions were 66 x 72.6 mm, so the capacity came out at 248 cc, and its construction was conventional. The top half was of iron, the rocker box forming an integral part of the cylinder head. Splayed pushrods ran up from the timing chest to rockers that lay across the head, under light-alloy access covers. Each pushrod had its own tube.

The prototype single had coil ignition, while the gearbox was bolted to the back of the crankcase.

The timing and gearbox-end covers were styled as one, while the usual Norton pressed-steel primary chaincase was fitted, along with a full rear chaincase. The engine unit was installed in a cradle frame with pivoted-fork rear suspension and telescopic front. An oil tank was in the usual right-hand position to service the dry-sump lubrication and was matched by a battery on the left. A toolbox was fitted on each side, while the exhaust system was on the right with a pear-shaped silencer. Wheels were conventional with offset hubs and 3.00 x 19in. tyres, a dualseat was fitted, and the finish was all silver-grey.

When the 1955 range was announced, four old friends had gone, but there were two new models. Those that went were the side-valve 16H and Big 4, the ohv model 18 and the trials 500T. New, but using an old model number, were the models 19R and 19S - rigid and sprung machines using a common 597 cc engine.

The new engine used the 82 x 113 mm dimensions of the Big 4 with the engine layout of the ES2. Externally, it was hard to tell the two sizes apart, and all were fitted with a light-alloy cylinder head and a Monobloc

Smart RAC patrolman at the salute on his Model 19 outfit.

carburettor. There was a new dualseat and handlebars, a boxed-in rear number plate, a smaller petrol tank of 2-3/4 gallons capacity, and thinner kneegrips. For the 19R alone there was a 4.00 x 18 in. rear tyre. The finish for all was as for the existing ES2. At the end of the year, the 19R was dropped.

In place of the dropped model, there was a new and smaller one, the model 50 of 348 cc. This was a dead ringer for the ES2, but its engine dimensions were 71 x 88 mm and it had a slightly higher compression ratio. All three singles were close to being identical; all had various detail engine improvements and a revised style. Part of this came from a combined toolbox and battery carrier, which was fitted into the left-hand subframe corner and was matched by a reshaped oil tank on the right.

The petrol tank size was increased again, and the headlamp shell deepened to carry the speedometer, along with the ammeter and light switch, in a panel attached to its top. The underslung pilot lamp was no more, while the horn button and dipswitch were combined on the right handlebar. The other major styling change came from the adoption of full-width, light-alloy hubs for both wheels, the brake sizes remaining as they were. There were also larger mudguards, a better prop stand, a flat-top dualseat and Armstrong rear units.

Black, chrome-plating and silver remained the finish, and during 1956 the gearbox type of all models was changed from the laid-down unit to the AMC type. The AMC gearbox was so-called because that group, which had ample gear-cutting facilities, had acquired the Norton company in 1953 and had chosen to modify the laid-down box a little, fitting the result to all their large singles and twins, whether they were AJS, Matchless or Norton models. The changes made the positive-stop mechanism more compact and introduced a new clutch-lift system.

For 1957, there was a new cylinder head with integral pushrod tunnels and a cast-in inlet flange. Inside, there were new cams. The frame was also improved and fitted with Girling rear units. At the front went a new hub and brake backplate, similar in form and size to that of the previous year.

There were a good number of minor alterations, among them a silencer of tubular form without tailpipe, and the direct mounting of the instruments and light switch into the headlamp shell. An optional air filter was listed. The finish changed in that the petrol tank was painted matt silver and then fitted with separate, chrome-plated side panels, which sat on plastic edge beads and were held in place by the badges and kneegrips. The old-style Norton footrests, of half-moon shape, were replaced by boring round rubbers.

Featherbed finale

There were no changes for 1958, at the end of which the 19S was dropped, but major revisions came in for 1959 with the adoption of the Featherbed frame and alternator electrics. The frame was the developed, production version of the type first used by the works racing singles in 1950. It was fully duplex with two main loops, the tubes of which crossed over just behind the headstock.

Of all-welded construction, including the subframe, it was fitted with the esteemed 'short' Roadholder front forks. The oil tank was revised to suit the frame form,

as was the combined toolbox and battery carrier, but the wheels remained as before. Essentially, the cycle parts were the same as those used by the twin-cylinder models.

The alternator was a Lucas RM15 and was mounted on the left-hand end of the crankshaft, inside the pressed-steel chaincase, whose outer was modified to accommodate it. The coil went under the enlarged petrol tank, and a points housing with auto-advance replaced the magneto, but utilised the same chain drive. Covers were added over the engine plates, and among the options were a full rear chaincase

The ES2 and Models 50 and 19 used common cycle parts for most years, including 1957, as here.

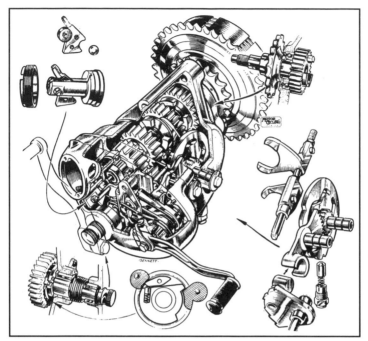

The AMC gearbox introduced in May 1956, but closely related to the 1935 Norton box, and to continue in use for many years.

and a sidecar kit. This kit included revised fork yokes, which gave sidecar trail, and stiffer suspension. To enhance the changes, there was a new finish with all painted parts in Forest green, but the traditional black and silver remained an option.

After such a major revision, little was altered for 1960, except for the internal gearbox ratios, plus the option of chrome-plated mudguards. There was more for 1961, however, when the slimline version of the Featherbed frame was adopted, this change having occurred to suit the twin-cylinder models with rear enclosure. The frame tubes were simply pulled closer together in the region of the dualseat nose.

The frame change enabled a narrower tank to be fitted, although this had a slightly larger capacity. The tank badges were changed to a longer style that incorporated small kneegrips and acted as a dividing line for a two-tone colour finish. With the new tank came a new, quickly-detachable dualseat, under which went the tools and electrical equipment. Both models had a two-tone finish with the lower petrol tank and mudguards in dove grey. The rest of the painted parts of the model 50 were in black, while those of the ES2 were in green. Chrome-plated mudguards were optional, as was a full chaincase, the sidecar kit and flat handlebars.

A 1958 Model 19 single whose engine was a little taller than that of the ES2 or Model 50.

Only the alternator was changed for 1962 - to an RM19 - the finish remaining as it was. However, for 1963, the colour was altered to off-white for the lower tank and mudguards with black for the remainder of the painted parts for both models.

Production of Norton machines was transferred to the AMC works in Plumstead at the end of 1962, and late in 1963 the singles line was dropped. The home market for

motorcycles was contracting at that time, and the sales accent was on twins for export. Few customers remained for the traditional single with an engine line that could be traced back to its Edwardian ancestors, even though it carried the Norton name.

Norton enthusiasts would have been happy for that to have been the end, but AMC did not leave it at that. In their financial difficulties, they looked for any avenue to shift stock, and for 1965 they reintroduced the models 50 and ES2 in Mk 2 forms. In truth, these were hybrids, only the forks and hubs coming from the Norton line, the engines and frames being AMC parts - the machines were simply the AJS models 16 and 18 or Matchless G3 and G80 fitted with Norton tank badges.

The engines were the final development of the AMC single, first seen in the mid 1930s, with ohv and conventional construction. The gearbox was the stock AMC type, and the chaincase a pair of light-

Major changes came in for 1959, including the Featherbed frame and alternator electrics as seen on this ES2.

Points housing for the coil ignition system adopted for 1959 in place of the magneto.

Smart Model 50 seen at the Banbury run in 1990.

alloy castings. Detail fittings were AMC or Norton to suit the assembly, and the finish was mainly black with a silver petrol tank.

The Mk 2 models were not popular with AMC or Norton fans, but they remained available for 1966 with just a change of tank lining and with transfers in place of the badges. Production ceased when AMC failed, and few shed tears at their passing.

To the Norton man, the marque's single was the epitome of the British machine, having adequate performance and the pull to roll up and down hills with ease. For many years, the 16H, Big 4, 18 and ES2 did just that, winning many friends and adherents to the marque. Their departure was mourned by many, but the machines live on, enabling classic enthusiasts of the 1990s once again to enjoy the thump of a Norton single.

Nicely restored slimline Featherbed Model 50 of 1961. Roadholding and brakes far exceeded the power of the machine.

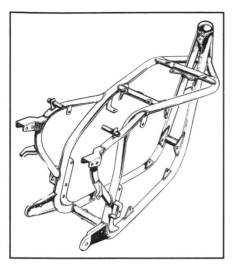

Slimline Featherbed frame as for the twins, the single-cylinder version being very similar.

The 1961 singles were fitted with a new style of petrol tank to enable two-tone finishes to be used. This is the ES2.

Drive-side of the 1961 ES2 showing the optional rear chaincase also available for the Model 50 and the twins.

From the side, it can be seen that the engine of this 1961 Model 50 did not reach up under the tank as much as the others.

Competition

To most people, Norton singles and competition mean road racing and the Manx model, but the more prosaic singles played their part in the firm's history as well. In the early days, both side- and overhead-valve machines broke records and won races, but these successes faded once the camshaft engines became available. A pushrod Norton had been the first 500 cc machine to put over 100 miles into the hour, in 1927, and to take the absolute record at 102 mph in the following year. However, when the figure rose to over 110 mph, in 1931, it was a camshaft Norton that achieved it.

Off-road, in trials, the Norton singles played their part during the 1930s, all models being available in a competition form from 1935 onwards. For sidecar trials, the camshaft engine was often used, together with sidecar wheel drive, and it was this expertise that led to the wartime Big 4 outfits used by the army.

Postwar, the firm used modified model 18 machines, which were so ill-suited to their task that not even skilled works riders could produce much in the way of results. In time,

Model 50 Norton in its final form, seen many years later and in very good order.

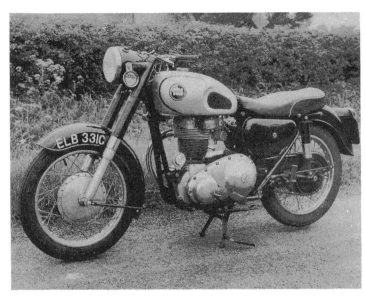

The Mk 2 ES2 and Model 50 models were badged AMC singles, also to be had with AJS or Matchless on the tank side.

there came the 500T and the situation changed, for the model was successful both during and after its production life. Most were used for trials, but a few went scrambling, where they enjoyed some success and worked well for the novice. The combination of good power delivery and Roadholder forks made the machine easy to ride, which was important to anyone with limited experience.

Both 500T and other ohv Norton singles also performed well at clubman level, in other off-road events such as grass-tracks and hill-climbs. Today, the trials Norton remains a popular choice for pre-1965 events.

The AMC clones were not a success with any marque enthusiast. All machines used Norton forks and hubs plus the common gearbox.

Competition version of the Norton single for 1938, complete with the strange silencer of that year.

The heavy and essentially standard Model 18 in trials form that Jack Williams had to campaign for the works in 1946.

Nice 500T outfit
seen at Daytona in
1991. Correct
period sidecar
matches well with
the pushrod single.

Restored 500T out in California. Owner claims to have found the last correct new toolbox left in
the world.

Interesting combination of Norton engine with AMC cylinder head for scrambles use.

Specifications

Model	16H & 2	Big 4	18 & 20	19	ES2 & 22	JE	50 & 55
years	1931-39 [1]	1931-39	1931-39	1931-39	1931-39 [2]	1931	1933-39
bore mm	79	82	79	79 [3]	79	71	71
stroke mm	100	120	100	120 [3]	100	88	88
capacity cc	490	634	490	588 [3]	490	348	348
comp. ratio	4.9	4.5 [4]	6.2	5.0 [5]	6.2 [6]		7.0
valves	sv	sv	ohv	ohv	ohv	ohv	ohv
carb type	76	76	76	76	76		76
carb size	1	1	1-1/16	1-1/16	1-1/16		1
ignition by	magneto	magneto	magneto	magneto	magneto	magneto	magneto
generator	dynamo	dynamo	dynamo	dynamo	dynamo	dynamo	dynamo
no.gears	3 [7]	3 [7]	3 [8]	3 [8]	3 [8]	3	4
top gear	4.64 [9]	4.64 [9]	4.42 [10]	4.42 [10]	4.42 [10]		5.16
forks	girder	girder	girder	girder	girder	girder	girder
frame	rigid	rigid	rigid	rigid	rigid [11]	rigid	rigid
petrol-gall	2.75	2.75	2.75	2.75 [12]	2.75 [13]	2.75	2.75
front tyre	26x3.25	26x3.25	26x3.25	26x3.25	26x3.25	26x3.25	26x3.25
rear tyre	26x3.25	26x3.25	26x3.25	26x3.25	26x3.25	26x3.25	26x3.25
front brake	7	7	7	7	7	7	7
rear brake	7	7	7	7	7	7	7
wheelbase in	54.5	54.5	54.5	54.5	54.5	54.5	54

[1] - model 2 to 1932
[2] - 1931 only for 22
[3] - 1933-82x113, 597cc
[4] - 1935-4.8
[5] - 1933-5.75
[6] - 1938-6.5
[7] - 1932-4 option, 1934-4
[8] - 1932-4 option, 1933-4
[9] - 1938-4.89
[10] - 1934-4.64
[11] - 1939-plunger option
[12] - 1935-3.25
[13] - 1937-3.25

Model	wd 16H	wd Big 4	16H	Big 4	18	ES2	ES2
years	1940-45	1940-45	1945-54	1947-54	1945-54	1947-58	1959-63
bore mm	79	82	79	82	79	79	79
stroke mm	100	120	100	120[1]	100	100	100
capacity cc	490	634	490	634[1]	490	490	490
comp. ratio	4.9	4.8	4.9	4.5	6.45[2]	6.45[3]	7.1
valves	sv	sv	sv	sv	ohv	ohv	ohv
carb type	276	276	276	276	276	276[4]	376
carb size	1	1	1	1	1-1/16	1-1/16	1-1/16
ignition by	magneto	magneto	magneto	magneto	magneto	magneto	coil
generator	dynamo	dynamo	dynamo	dynamo	dynamo	dynamo	alt
no.gears	4	4	4	4	4	4	4
top gear	5.28	6.39	4.89[5]	5.46[6]	4.64[7]	4.64[7]	4.75
forks	girder	girder	girder[8]	teles	girder[8]	teles	teles
frame	rigid	rigid	rigid[9]	rigid[9]	rigid	plunger[10]	s/a
petrol-gall	2.75	2.75	2.75[11]	2.75[11]	2.75[11]	2.75[12]	3.5[13]
front tyre	3.25x19		3.25x19	3.25x19	3.25x19	3.25x19	3.00x19
rear tyre	3.25x19		3.25x19	3.25x19	3.25x19	3.25x19	3.50x19
front brake	7	7	7[14]	7[14]	7[14]	7[14]	8
rear brake	7	7	7	7	7	7	7
wheelbase in	54.5		54.5	54.5	54.5	54.5[15]	55.5

[1] - 1948-113, 597cc
[2] - 1952-6.6
[3] - 1952-6.6, 1955-6.8, 1956-7.1
[4] - 1955-376
[5] - 1953-5.00
[6] - 1953-5.60
[7] - 1953-4.75
[8] - 1947-teles
[9] - some plunger
[10] - 1953-s/a
[11] - 1951-3.5
[12] - 1951-3.5, 1955-2.75, 1956-3.25
[13] - 1961-3.62
[14] - 1954-8
[15] - 1957-57

Model	500T	19R	19S	50	50	ES2 Mk2	50 Mk2
years	1949-54	1955	1955-58	1956-58	1959-63	1965-66	1965-66
bore mm	79	82	82	71	71	86	72
stroke mm	100	113	113	88	88	85.5	85.5
capacity cc	490	597	597	348	348	497	348
comp. ratio	6.0	6.2	6.2 [1]	7.3	7.3	7.3	9.0
valves	ohv	ohv	ohv	ohv	ohv	ohv	ohv
carb type	276	376	376	376	376	389	389
carb size	1-1/16	1-1/16	1-1/16	1	1	1-1/8	1-1/8
ignition by	magneto	magneto	magneto	magneto	coil	coil	coil
generator		dynamo	dynamo	dynamo	alt	alt	alt
no.gears	4	4	4	4	4	4	4
top gear	5.51	5.28	4.52	5.28	5.28	4.79	5.51
forks	teles	teles	teles	teles	teles	teles	teles
frame	rigid	rigid	s/a	s/a	s/a	s/a	s/a
petrol-gall	2.5	2.75	2.75 [2]	3.25	3.5 [3]	4	4
front tyre	2.75x21	3.25x19	3.25x19	3.25x19	3.00x19	3.25x18	3.25x18
rear tyre	4.00x19	4.00x18	3.25x19	3.25x19	3.50x19	3.50x18	3.25x18
front brake	7	8	8	8	8	8	8
rear brake	7	7	7	7	7	7	7
wheelbase in	53	54.5	54.5 [4]	54.5 [4]	55.5		

[1] - 1956-6.4   [2] - 1956-3.25   [3] - 1961-3.62
[4] - 1957-57